Key Facts™ on

Jordan

~*Essential Information on Jordan*~

By Patrick W. Nee

The Internationalist®

www.internationalist.com

The Internationalist®

International Business, Investment, and Travel

Published by:

The Internationalist Publishing Company

96 Walter Street/ Suite 200

Boston, MA 02131, USA

Tel: 617-354-7722

www.internationalist.com

PN@internationalist.com

Table Of Contents

Chapter 1: Background

Following World War I and the dissolution of the Ottoman Empire, the League of Nations awarded Britain the mandate to govern much of the Middle East. Britain demarcated a semi-autonomous region of Transjordan from Palestine in the early 1920s. The area gained its independence in 1946 and thereafter became The Hashemite Kingdom of Jordan. The country's long-time ruler, King HUSSEIN (1953-99), successfully navigated competing pressures from the major powers (US, USSR, and UK), various Arab states, Israel, and a large internal Palestinian population. Jordan lost the West Bank to Israel in the 1967 Six-Day War. King HUSSEIN in 1988 permanently relinquished Jordanian claims to the West Bank; in 1994 he signed a peace treaty with Israel. King ABDALLAH II, King HUSSEIN's eldest son, assumed the throne following his father's death in 1999. He implemented modest political and economic reforms, but in the wake of the "Arab Revolution" across the Middle East, Jordanians continue to press for further political liberalization, government reforms, and economic improvements.

Chapter 2: Geography

Location:

> Middle East, northwest of Saudi Arabia, between Israel (to the west) and Iraq

Geographic coordinates:

> 31 00 N, 36 00 E

Map references:

> Middle East

Area:

> total: 89,342 sq km
>
> country comparison to the world: 112
>
> land: 88,802 sq km
>
> water: 540 sq km

Area - comparative:

> slightly smaller than Indiana

Land boundaries:

> total: 1,635 km
>
> border countries: Iraq 181 km, Israel 238 km, Saudi Arabia 744 km, Syria 375 km, West Bank 97 km

Coastline:

> 26 km

Maritime claims:

> territorial sea: 3 nm

Climate:

mostly arid desert; rainy season in west (November to April)

Terrain:

mostly desert plateau in east, highland area in west; Great Rift Valley separates East and West Banks of the Jordan River

Elevation extremes:

lowest point: Dead Sea -408 m

highest point: Jabal Umm ad Dami 1,854 m

Natural resources:

phosphates, potash, shale oil

Land use:

arable land: 1.97%

permanent crops: 0.95%

other: 97.08% (2011)

Irrigated land:

788.6 sq km (2004)

Total renewable water resources:

0.94 cu km (2011)

Freshwater withdrawal (domestic/industrial/agricultural):

total: 0.94 cu km/yr (31%/4%/65%)

per capita: 166 cu m/yr (2005)

Natural hazards:

droughts; periodic earthquakes

Environment - current issues:

limited natural freshwater resources; deforestation; overgrazing; soil erosion; desertification

Environment - international agreements:

party to: Biodiversity, Climate Change, Climate Change-Kyoto Protocol, Desertification, Endangered Species, Hazardous Wastes, Law of the Sea, Marine Dumping, Ozone Layer Protection, Wetlands signed, but not ratified: none of the selected agreements

Geography - note:

strategic location at the head of the Gulf of Aqaba and as the Arab country that shares the longest border with Israel and the occupied West Bank

Chapter 3: People and Society

Nationality:

noun: Jordanian(s)

adjective: Jordanian

Ethnic groups:

Arab 98%, Circassian 1%, Armenian 1%

Languages:

Arabic (official), English (widely understood among upper and middle classes)

Religions:

Sunni Muslim 92% (official), Christian 6% (majority Greek Orthodox, but some Greek and Roman Catholics, Syrian Orthodox, Coptic Orthodox, Armenian Orthodox, and Protestant denominations), other 2% (several small Shia Muslim and Druze populations) (2001 est.)

Population:

6,482,081 (July 2013 est.)

country comparison to the world: 104

Age structure:

0-14 years: 34.6% (male 1,154,791/female 1,089,901)

15-24 years: 19.9% (male 661,516/female 625,311)

25-54 years: 36.2% (male 1,181,882/female 1,164,957)

55-64 years: 4.3% (male 133,371/female 142,636)

65 years and over: 5.1% (male 158,514/female 169,202) (2013 est.)

Median age:

total: 22.6 years

male: 22.2 years

female: 22.9 years (2013 est.)

Population growth rate:

0.14% (2013 est.)

country comparison to the world: 181

Birth rate:

26.23 births/1,000 population (2013 est.)

country comparison to the world: 51

Death rate:

2.8 deaths/1,000 population (2013 est.)

country comparison to the world: 220

Net migration rate:

-22.02 migrant(s)/1,000 population (2013 est.)

country comparison to the world: 220

Urbanization:

urban population: 79% of total population (2010)

rate of urbanization: 1.6% annual rate of change (2010-15 est.)

Major cities - population:

AMMAN (capital) 1.088 million (2009)

Sex ratio:

at birth: 1.06 male(s)/female

0-14 years: 1.06 male(s)/female

15-24 years: 1.06 male(s)/female

25-54 years: 1.02 male(s)/female

55-64 years: 0.93 male(s)/female

65 years and over: 0.95 male(s)/female

total population: 1.03 male(s)/female (2013 est.)

Maternal mortality rate:

63 deaths/100,000 live births (2010)

country comparison to the world: 97

Infant mortality rate:

total: 15.26 deaths/1,000 live births

country comparison to the world: 108

male: 15.89 deaths/1,000 live births

female: 14.59 deaths/1,000 live births (2013 est.)

Life expectancy at birth:

total population: 80.3 years

country comparison to the world: 29

male: 78.91 years

female: 81.77 years (2013 est.)

Total fertility rate:

3.32 children born/woman (2013 est.)

country comparison to the world: 50

Health expenditures:

8% of GDP (2010)

country comparison to the world: 59

Physicians density:

2.45 physicians/1,000 population (2009)

Hospital bed density:

1.8 beds/1,000 population (2010)

Drinking water source:

improved:

urban: 98% of population

rural: 92% of population

total: 97% of population

unimproved:

urban: 2% of population

rural: 8% of population

total: 3% of population (2010 est.)

Sanitation facility access:

improved:

urban: 98% of population

rural: 98% of population

> *total*: 98% of population

unimproved:

> *urban*: 2% of population

> *rural*: 2% of population

> *total*: 2% of population (2010 est.)

HIV/AIDS - adult prevalence rate:

> less than 0.1% (2001 est.)

> country comparison to the world: 132

HIV/AIDS - people living with HIV/AIDS:

> 600 (2007 est.)

> country comparison to the world: 149

HIV/AIDS - deaths:

> fewer than 500 (2003 est.)

> country comparison to the world: 88

Obesity - adult prevalence rate:

> 30% (2008)

> country comparison to the world: 28

Children under the age of 5 years underweight:

> 1.9% (2009)

> country comparison to the world: 119

Education expenditures:

> NA

Literacy:

> definition: age 15 and over can read and write

total population: 92.6%

male: 95.8%

female: 89.2% (2010 est.)

School life expectancy (primary to tertiary education):

total: 13 years

male: 13 years

female: 13 years (2008)

Unemployment, youth ages 15-24:

total: 29.9%

country comparison to the world: 26

male: 26.2%

female: 46.8% (2011)

Chapter 4: Government and Key Leaders

Country name:

conventional long form: Hashemite Kingdom of
Jordan

conventional short form: Jordan

local long form: Al Mamlakah al Urduniyah al
Hashimiyah

local short form: Al Urdun

former: Transjordan

Government type:

constitutional monarchy

Capital:

name: Amman

geographic coordinates: 31 57 N, 35 56 E

time difference: UTC+2 (7 hours ahead of
Washington, DC during Standard Time)

daylight saving time: +1hr, begins first Friday in
April; ends last Friday in October

note: Jordan remains on DST following a decision by
the government to cancel a change back to Standard
Time in October 2012; DST currently scheduled to
end the fourth Friday in October

Administrative divisions:

12 governorates (muhafazat, singular - muhafazah); Ajlun, Al 'Aqabah, Al Balqa', Al Karak, Al Mafraq, 'Amman, At Tafilah, Az Zarqa', Irbid, Jarash, Ma'an, Madaba

Independence:

25 May 1946 (from League of Nations mandate under British administration)

National holiday:

Independence Day, 25 May (1946)

Constitution:

1 January 1952; amended many times

Legal system:

mixed legal system of civil law and Islamic religious law; judicial review of legislative acts in a specially provided High Tribunal

International law organization participation:

has not submitted an ICJ jurisdiction declaration; accepts ICCt jurisdiction

Suffrage:

18 years of age; universal

Executive branch:

chief of state: King ABDALLAH II (since 7 February 1999); Crown Prince HUSSEIN (born 28 June 1994), eldest son of King ABDALLAH II head of government: Prime Minister Abdullah NSOUR (since 11 October 2012)

cabinet: Cabinet appointed by the prime minister in consultation with the monarch; note - a new cabinet was sworn in 30 March 2013

elections: the monarchy is hereditary; prime minister appointed by the monarch

Legislative branch:

bicameral National Assembly or Majlis al-'Umma consists of the Senate, also called the House of Notables or Majlis al-Ayan (60 seats; members appointed by the monarch to serve four-year terms) and the Chamber of Deputies, also called the House of Representatives or Majlis al-Nuwaab (150 seats; 123 members elected using the single, non-transferable vote system in multi-member districts, and 27 seats elected using a closed national list system based on proportional representation; all legislators serve four-year terms); note - the new electoral law enacted in July 2012 allocated an additional 10 seats (6 seats added to the number reserved for women, bringing the total to 15; 2 additional seats for Amman; and 1 seat each for the cities of Zarqa and Irbid; unchanged are 9 seats reserved for Christian candidates, 9 for Bedouin candidates, and 3 for Jordanians of Chechen or Circassian descent

elections: Chamber of Deputies - last held on 23 January 2013 (next election NA); note - the King dissolved the previous Chamber of Deputies in November 2012, midway through the parliamentary term

election results: Chamber of Deputies - percent of vote by party - NA; seats by party - 27 elected on closed national list to include: Islamic Centrist Party 3, Nation 2, National Union 2, Stronger Jordan 2, Ahl al-Himma 1, Al-Bayyan 1, Citizenship 1, Construction 1, Cooperation 1, Dawn 1, Dignity 1, Free Voice 1, Labor and Trade 1, National Accord Youth Block 1, National Action 1, National Current 1 (member resigned in February 2013), National Unity 1, Nobel Jerusalem 1, Salvation 1, The People 1, Unified Front 1, Voice of Nation 1; other 123; note - the IAF boycotted the election

Judicial branch:

Court of Cassation (Supreme Court); Constitutional Court

Political parties and leaders:

Ahl al-Himma; Al-Bayyan; Al-Hayah Jordanian Pary [Zahier AMR]; Arab Ba'ath Socialist Party [Akram al-HIMSI]; Ba'ath Arab Progressive Party [Fuad DABBOUR]; Citizenship; Construction; Cooperation; Dawn; Democratic People's Party [Ablah ABU ULBAH]; Democratic Popular Unity Party [Sa'id DIAB]; Dignity; Du'a Party [Muhammed ABU BAKR]; Free Voice; Islamic Action Front or IAF [Hamzah MANSOUR]; Islamic Centrist Party [Muhammad al-HAJ]; Jordanian Communist Party [Munir HAMARNAH]; Jordanian National Party [Muna ABU BAKR]; Jordanian United Front [Amjad al-MAJALI]; Labor and Trade; Nation; National Accord Youth Block; National Action; National Constitution Party [Ahmad al-SHUNAQ]; National Current Party [Abd al-Hadi al-MAJALI]; National Movement for Direct Democracy [Muhammad al-QAQ]; National Union; National Unity; Nobel Jerusalem; Risalah Party [Hazem QASHOU]; Salvation; Stronger Jordan; The Direct Democratic Nationalists Movement Party [Nash'at KHALIFAH]; The People; Unified Front; United Front; Voice of the Nation

Political pressure groups and leaders:

15 April Movement [Mohammad SUNEID, chairman]; 24 March Movement [Mu'az al-KHAWALIDAH, Abdel Rahman HASANEIN, spokespersons]; 1952 Constitution Movement; Anti-Normalization Committee [Hamzah MANSOUR, chairman]; Economic and Social Association of Retired Servicemen and Veterans or ESARSV [Abdulsalam al-HASSANAT, chairman]; Group of 36; Higher Coordination Committee of Opposition Parties [Said DIAB]; Higher National Committee for Military Retirees or HNCMR [Ali al-HABASHNEH, chairman]; Hirak; Jordan Bar Association [Saleh al-ARMUTI, chairman]; Jordanian Campaign for Change or Jayin; Jordanian Muslim Brotherhood [Dr. Hamam SAID, controller general]; Jordanian Press Association [Sayf al-SHARIF, president]; National Front for Reform or NFR [Ahmad OBEIDAT, chairman]; Popular Gathering for Reform; Professional Associations Council [Abd al-Hadi al-FALAHAT, chairman]; Sons of Jordan

International organization participation:

ABEDA, AFESD, AMF, CAEU, CD, CICA, EBRD, FAO, G-11, G-77, IAEA, IBRD, ICAO, ICC (national committees), ICRM, IDA, IDB, IFAD, IFC,

IFRCS, ILO, IMF, IMO, Interpol, IOC, IOM, IPU, ISO, ITSO, ITU, ITUC (NGOs), LAS, MIGA, MINUSTAH, MONUSCO, NAM, OIC, OPCW, OSCE (partner), PCA, UN, UNAMID, UNCTAD, UNESCO, UNHCR, UNIDO, UNISFA, UNMIL, UNMISS, UNOCI, UNRWA, UNWTO, UPU, WCO, WFTU (NGOs), WHO, WIPO, WMO, WTO

Diplomatic representation in the US:

chief of mission: Ambassador Alia Hatough-BOURAN

chancery: 3504 International Drive NW, Washington, DC 20008

telephone: [1] (202) 966-2664

FAX: [1] (202) 966-3110

Diplomatic representation from the US:

chief of mission: Ambassador Stuart E. JONES

embassy: Abdoun, Al-Umawyeen St., Amman

mailing address: P. O. Box 354, Amman 11118 Jordan; Unit 70200, Box 5, DPO AE 09892-0200

telephone: [962] (6) 590-6000

FAX: [962] (6) 592-0163

Key Leaders:

King	ABDALLAH II
Prime Min.	Abdullah NSOUR

Min. of Agriculture	Hazem NASSER
Min. of Awqaf & Islamic Affairs	Muhammad al-QUDAH
Min. of Culture	Barakat AWAJAN
Min. of Defense	Abdullah NSOUR
Min. of Education	Mohammad WAHSH
Min. of Energy & Mineral Resources	Malek KABARITI
Min. of the Environment	Mujalli MHAILAN
Min. of Finance	Umayya TOUKAN
Min. of Foreign Affairs & Expatriate Affairs	Nasser JUDEH
Min. of Health	Mujalli MHAILAN
Min. of Higher Education & Scientific Research	Amin MAHMOUD
Min. of Information & Communication Technology	Hatem Hafez Al HALAWANI
Min. of Industry, Trade, & Supply	Hatem Hafez Al HALAWANI
Min. of Interior	Hussein MAJALI
Min. of Justice	Ahmad ZIADAT
Min. of Labor	Nidal Mardi QATAMIN

Min. of Municipal Affairs	Hussein MAJALI
Min. of Parliamentary Affairs	Mohammad MOMANI
Min. of Planning & Intl. Cooperation	Ibrahim SAIF
Min. of Political Development	Mohammad MOMANI
Min. of Public Sector Development	Khleif al-KHAWALDEH
Min. of Public Works & Housing	Walid MASRI
Min. of Social Development	Reem ABU HASSAN
Min. of Tourism & Antiquities	Ibrahim SAIF
Min. of Transportation	Nidal Mardi QATAMIN
Min. of Water & Irrigation	Hazem NASSER
Min. of State for Media Affairs & Communication	Mohammad MOMANI
Min. of State for Prime-Ministerial Affairs	Ahmad ZIADAT
Governor, Central Bank of Jordan	Mohammad Said SHAHEEN

Ambassador to the US	Alia Hatough-BOURAN
Permanent Representative to the UN, New York	ZEID Ra'ad Zeid al-Hussein

Flag description:

three equal horizontal bands of black (top), representing the Abbassid Caliphate, white, representing the Ummayyad Caliphate, and green, representing the Fatimid Caliphate; a red isosceles triangle on the hoist side, representing the Great Arab Revolt of 1916, and bearing a small white seven-pointed star symbolizing the seven verses of the opening Sura (Al-Fatiha) of the Holy Koran; the seven points on the star represent faith in One God, humanity, national spirit, humility, social justice, virtue, and aspirations; design is based on the Arab Revolt flag of World War I

National symbol(s):

eagle

National anthem:

name: "As-salam al-malaki al-urdoni" (Long Live the King of Jordan)

lyrics/music: Abdul-Mone'm al-RIFAI'/Abdul-Qader al-TANEER

<u>note</u>: adopted 1946; the shortened version of the anthem is used most commonly, while the full version is reserved for special occasions

Chapter 5: Economy

Economy - overview:

Jordan's economy is among the smallest in the Middle East, with insufficient supplies of water, oil, and other natural resources, underlying the government's heavy reliance on foreign assistance. Other economic challenges for the government include chronic high rates of poverty, unemployment, inflation, and a large budget deficit. Since assuming the throne in 1999, King ABDALLAH has implemented significant economic reforms, such as opening the trade regime, privatizing state-owned companies, and eliminating some fuel subsidies, which in the last decade spurred economic growth by attracting foreign investment and creating some jobs. The global economic slowdown and regional turmoil, however, have depressed Jordan's GDP growth, impacting export-oriented sectors, construction, and tourism. In 2011 and 2012, the government approved two economic relief packages and a budgetary supplement, meant to improve the living conditions for the middle and poor classes. Jordan's finances have also been strained by a series of natural gas pipeline attacks in Egypt, causing

Jordan to substitute more expensive diesel imports, primarily from Saudi Arabia, to generate electricity. Jordan is currently exploring nuclear power generation in addition to the exploitation of abundant oil shale reserves and renewable technologies to forestall energy shortfalls. In 2012, to correct budgetary and balance of payments imbalances, Jordan entered into a $2.1 billion, multiple year International Monetary Fund Stand-By Arrangement. Jordan's financial sector has been relatively isolated from the international financial crisis because of its limited exposure to overseas capital markets. Jordan will continue to depend heavily on foreign assistance to finance the deficit in 2013.

GDP (purchasing power parity):

$38.67 billion (2012 est.)

country comparison to the world: 105

$37.54 billion (2011 est.)

$36.59 billion (2010 est.)

note: data are in 2012 US dollars

GDP (official exchange rate):

$31.35 billion (2012 est.)

GDP - real growth rate:

3% (2012 est.)

country comparison to the world: 107

2.6% (2011 est.)

2.3% (2010 est.)

GDP - per capita (PPP):

$6,000 (2012 est.)

country comparison to the world: 146

$6,000 (2011 est.)

$6,000 (2010 est.)

note: data are in 2012 US dollars

GDP - composition by sector:

agriculture: 4.5%

industry: 30.9%

services: 64.6% (2012 est.)

Labor force:

1.824 million (2012 est.)

country comparison to the world: 126

Labor force - by occupation:

agriculture: 2.7%

industry: 20%

services: 77.4% (2007 est.)

Unemployment rate:

12.3% (2012 est.)

country comparison to the world: 129

12.3% (2011 est.)

note: official rate; unofficial rate is approximately
30%

Population below poverty line:

14.2% (2002)

Household income or consumption by percentage share:

lowest 10%: 3.4%

highest 10%: 28.7% (2010 est.)

Distribution of family income - Gini index:

39.7 (2007)

country comparison to the world: 62

36.4 (1997)

Investment (gross fixed):

28.9% of GDP (2012 est.)

country comparison to the world: 24

Budget:

revenues: $6.378 billion

expenditures: $8.39 billion (2012 est.)

Taxes and other revenues:

20.3% of GDP (2012 est.)

country comparison to the world: 160

Budget surplus (+) or deficit (-):

-6.4% of GDP (2012 est.)

country comparison to the world: 183

Public debt:

75% of GDP (2012 est.)

country comparison to the world: 32

70.7% of GDP (2011 est.)

note: data cover central government debt, and include debt instruments issued (or owned) by government entities other than the treasury; the data include treasury debt held by foreign entities; the data exclude debt issued by subnational entities, as well as intra-governmental debt; intra-governmental debt consists of treasury borrowings from surpluses in the social funds, such as for retirement, medical care, and unemployment; debt instruments for the social funds are not sold at public auctions

Inflation rate (consumer prices):

4.3% (2012 est.)

country comparison to the world: 119

4.4% (2011 est.)

Central bank discount rate:

0.3% (31 December 2010 est.)

country comparison to the world: 75

4.75% (31 December 2009 est.)

Commercial bank prime lending rate:

8.68% (31 December 2012 est.)

country comparison to the world: 113

8.22% (31 December 2011 est.)

Stock of narrow money:

$11.15 billion (31 December 2012 est.)

country comparison to the world: 76

$10.26 billion (31 December 2011 est.)

Stock of broad money:

$38.61 billion (31 December 2012 est.)

country comparison to the world: 72

$34.02 billion (31 December 2011 est.)

Stock of domestic credit:

$33.27 billion (31 December 2012 est.)

country comparison to the world: 70

$30.8 billion (31 December 2011 est.)

Market value of publicly traded shares:

$27 billion (31 December 2012)

country comparison to the world: 58

$27.18 billion (31 December 2011)

$30.86 billion (31 December 2010)

Agriculture - products:

citrus, tomatoes, cucumbers, olives, strawberries, stone fruits; sheep, poultry, dairy

Industries:

clothing, fertilizers, potash, phosphate mining, pharmaceuticals, petroleum refining, cement, inorganic chemicals, light manufacturing, tourism

Industrial production growth rate:

0.2% (2012 est.)

country comparison to the world: 142

Current account balance:

$-3.359 billion (2012 est.)

country comparison to the world: 151

$-2.871 billion (2011 est.)

Exports:

$7.836 billion (2012 est.)

country comparison to the world: 101

$7.974 billion (2011 est.)

Exports - commodities:

clothing, fertilizers, potash, phosphates, vegetables, pharmaceuticals

Exports - partners:

US 15.4%, Iraq 15%, India 12.9%, Saudi Arabia 9.4%, Lebanon 4.4% (2011)

Imports:

$20.83 billion (2012 est.)

country comparison to the world: 75

$18.76 billion (2011 est.)

Imports - commodities:

crude oil, machinery, transport equipment, iron, cereals

Imports - partners:

Saudi Arabia 22.1%, China 9.8%, US 6.4%, Italy 5.1%, Germany 4.5% (2011)

Reserves of foreign exchange and gold:

$10.7 billion (31 December 2012 est.)

country comparison to the world: 71

$12.11 billion (31 December 2011 est.)

Debt - external:

$6.065 billion (30 November 2012 est.)

country comparison to the world: 105

$5.61 billion (31 December 2011 est.)

Stock of direct foreign investment - at home:

$24.63 billion (31 December 2012 est.)

country comparison to the world: 66

$22.91 billion (31 December 2011 est.)

Stock of direct foreign investment - abroad:

$NA

Exchange rates:

Jordanian dinars (JOD) per US dollar -

0.71 (2012 est.)

0.71 (2011 est.)

0.71 (2010 est.)

0.71 (2009)

0.71 (2008)

Fiscal year:

calendar year

Chapter 6: Energy

Electricity - production:

14.64 billion kWh (2011 est.)

country comparison to the world: 86

Electricity - consumption:

13.54 billion kWh (2011 est.)

country comparison to the world: 79

Electricity - exports:

86 million kWh (2011 est.)

country comparison to the world: 74

Electricity - imports:

1.738 billion kWh (2011 est.)

country comparison to the world: 54

Electricity - installed generating capacity:

3.14 million kW (2010 est.)

country comparison to the world: 87

Electricity - from fossil fuels:

99.3% of total installed capacity (2009 est.)

country comparison to the world: 58

Electricity - from nuclear fuels:

0% of total installed capacity (2009 est.)

country comparison to the world: 116

Electricity - from hydroelectric plants:

0.5% of total installed capacity (2009 est.)

country comparison to the world: 145

Electricity - from other renewable sources:

0.2% of total installed capacity (2009 est.)

country comparison to the world: 89

Crude oil - production:

20 bbl/day (2011 est.)

country comparison to the world: 102

Crude oil - exports:

0 bbl/day (2011 est.)

country comparison to the world: 133

Crude oil - imports:

29,310 bbl/day (2009 est.)

country comparison to the world: 65

Crude oil - proved reserves:

1 million bbl (1 January 2012 es)

country comparison to the world: 100

Refined petroleum products - production:

79,190 bbl/day (2008 est.)

country comparison to the world: 80

Refined petroleum products - consumption:

107,000 bbl/day (2011 est.)

country comparison to the world: 76

Refined petroleum products - exports:

0 bbl/day (2008 est.)

country comparison to the world: 188

Refined petroleum products - imports:

18,620 bbl/day (2008 est.)

country comparison to the world: 107

Natural gas - production:

226.5 million cu m (2011 est.)

country comparison to the world: 76

Natural gas - consumption:

1.4 billion cu m (2011 est.)

country comparison to the world: 84

Natural gas - exports:

0 cu m (2010 est.)

country comparison to the world: 124

Natural gas - imports:

793 million cu m (2011 est.)

country comparison to the world: 63

Natural gas - proved reserves:

6.031 billion cu m (1 January 2012 es)

country comparison to the world: 86

Carbon dioxide emissions from consumption of energy:

19.07 million Mt (2010 est.)

country comparison to the world: 85

Chapter 7: Communications

Telephones - main lines in use:

465,400 (2011)

country comparison to the world: 102

Telephones - mobile cellular:

7.483 million (2011)

country comparison to the world: 93

Telephone system:

general assessment: service has improved recently
with increased use of digital switching equipment;
microwave radio relay transmission and coaxial and
fiber-optic cable are employed on trunk lines;
growing mobile-cellular usage in both urban and rural
areas is reducing use of fixed-line services

domestic: 1995 telecommunications law opened all
non-fixed-line services to private competition; in
2005, monopoly over fixed-line services terminated
and the entire telecommunications sector was opened
to competition; currently multiple mobile-cellular
providers with subscribership reaching 115 per 100
persons in 2011

international: country code - 962; landing point for
the Fiber-Optic Link Around the Globe (FLAG) FEA

and FLAG Falcon submarine cable networks; satellite earth stations - 33 (3 Intelsat, 1 Arabsat, and 29 land and maritime Inmarsat terminals); fiber-optic cable to Saudi Arabia and microwave radio relay link with Egypt and Syria; participant in Medarabtel (2011)

Broadcast media:

radio and TV dominated by the government-owned Jordan Radio and Television Corporation (JRTV) that operates a main network, a sports network, a film network, and a satellite channel; first independent TV broadcaster aired in 2007; international satellite TV and Israeli and Syrian TV broadcasts are available; roughly 30 radio stations with JRTV operating the main government-owned station; transmissions of multiple international radio broadcasters are available (2007)

Internet country code:

.jo

Internet hosts:

69,473 (2012)

country comparison to the world: 89

Internet users:

1.642 million (2009)

country comparison to the world: 78

Chapter 8: Transportation

Airports:

18 (2012)

country comparison to the world: 139

Airports - with paved runways:

total: 16

over 3,047 m: 8

2,438 to 3,047 m: 5

1,524 to 2,437 m: 2

914 to 1,523 m: 1 (2012)

Airports - with unpaved runways:

total: 2

under 914 m: 2 (2012)

Heliports:

1 (2012)

Pipelines:

gas 439 km; oil 49 km (2010)

Railways:

total: 507 km

country comparison to the world: 111

narrow gauge: 507 km 1.050-m gauge (2008)

Roadways:

total: 7,891 km

country comparison to the world: 142

paved: 7,891 km (2009)

Merchant marine:

total: 12

country comparison to the world: 106

by type: cargo 4, passenger/cargo 6, petroleum tanker 1, roll on/roll off 1

foreign-owned: 2 (UAE 2)

registered in other countries: 16 (Bahamas 2, Egypt 2, Indonesia 1, Panama 11) (2010)

Ports and terminals:

Al 'Aqabah

Chapter 9: Military

Military branches:

> Jordanian Armed Forces (JAF): Royal Jordanian Land Force (RJLF), Royal Jordanian Navy, Royal Jordanian Air Force (Al-Quwwat al-Jawwiya al-Malakiya al-Urduniya, RJAF), Special Operations Command (Socom); Public Security Directorate (normally falls under Ministry of Interior, but comes under JAF in wartime or crisis) (2013)

Military service age and obligation:

> 17 years of age for voluntary male military service; initial service term 2 years, with option to reenlist for 18 years; conscription at age 18 suspended in 1999; women not subject to conscription, but can volunteer to serve in noncombat military positions in the Royal Jordanian Arab Army Women's Corps and RJAF (2013)

Manpower available for military service:

> males age 16-49: 1,674,260
> females age 16-49: 1,611,315 (2010 est.)

Manpower fit for military service:

> males age 16-49: 1,439,192
> females age 16-49: 1,384,500 (2010 est.)

Manpower reaching militarily significant age annually:

male: 73,574

female: 69,420 (2010 est.)

Military expenditures:

9.5% of GDP (2012)

country comparison to the world: 4

Chapter 10: Transnational Issues

Disputes - international:

2004 Agreement settles border dispute with Syria pending demarcation

Refugees and internally displaced persons:

refugees (country of origin): 1,979,580 (Palestinian refugees (UNRWA)) (2011); 29,191 (Iraq) (2012); 448,370 (Syria) (2013)

Map of Jordan

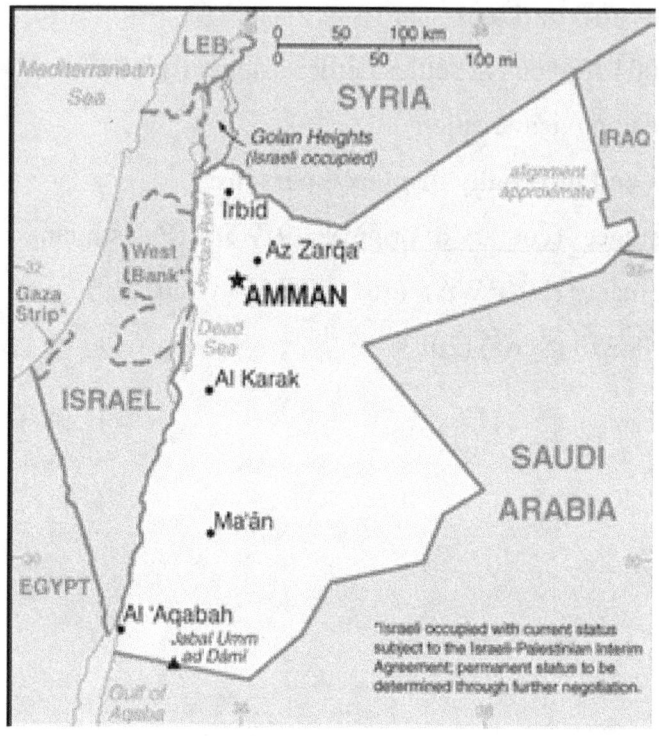

Other Key Facts™ Titles

Key Facts on Syria

Key Facts on China

Key Facts on Qatar

Key Facts on India

Key Facts on Germany

Key Facts on Argentina

Key Facts on Russia

Key Facts on North Korea

Key Facts on Brazil

Key Facts on Italy

Key Facts on the United Arab Emirates

Key Facts on the European Union

Key Facts on Pakistan

Key Facts on Saudi Arabia

Key Facts on Cyprus

Key Facts on Malaysia

Key Facts on Vietnam

Key Facts on Hong Kong

All Key Facts™ Titles are Available at

www.Amazon.com

THE INTERNATIONALIST®

2013

WWW.INTERNATIONALIST.COM